*Look for me by*
*moonlight*

Look for me by
moonlight

# THE Highwayman

ALFRED NOYES

THE *Highwayman*

WITH ILLUSTRATIONS BY

# MURRAY KIMBER

KCP POETRY
*An Imprint of Kids Can Press*

*The wind* was a torrent
    of darkness among the gusty trees.
The moon was a ghostly galleon
    tossed upon cloudy seas.
The road was a ribbon of moonlight
    over the purple moor,

And the highwayman came riding —
Riding — riding —
The highwayman came riding,
up to the old inn-door.

He'd a French cocked-hat on his forehead,
    a bunch of lace at his chin,
A coat of the claret velvet, and breeches
    of brown doe-skin.
They fitted with never a wrinkle.
    His boots were up to the thigh.
And he rode with a jewelled twinkle,
        His pistol butts a-twinkle,
His rapier hilt a-twinkle, under the jewelled sky.

Over the cobbles he clattered and
    clashed in the dark inn-yard.
He tapped with his whip on the shutters,
    but all was locked and barred.
He whistled a tune to the window,
    and who should be waiting there
But the landlord's black-eyed daughter,
        Bess, the landlord's daughter,
Plaiting a dark red love-knot
    into her long black hair.

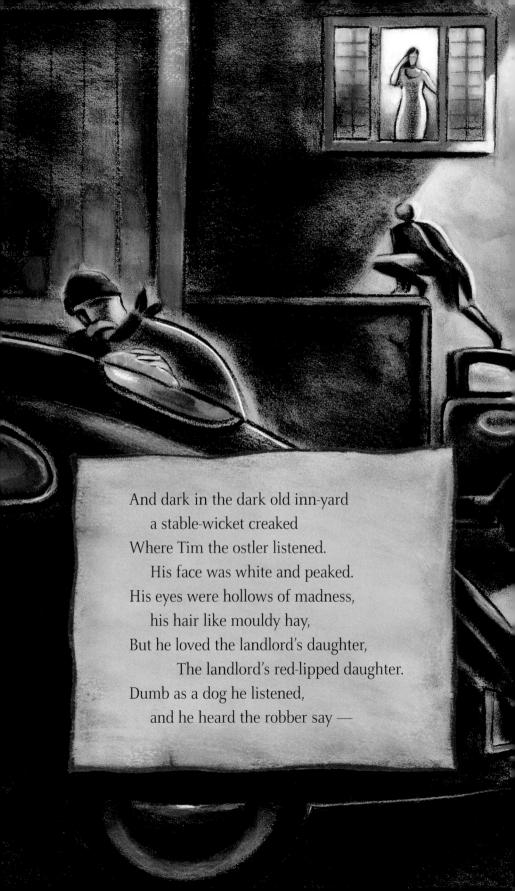

And dark in the dark old inn-yard
　　a stable-wicket creaked
Where Tim the ostler listened.
　　His face was white and peaked.
His eyes were hollows of madness,
　　his hair like mouldy hay,
But he loved the landlord's daughter,
　　The landlord's red-lipped daughter.
Dumb as a dog he listened,
　　and he heard the robber say —

"One kiss, my bonny sweetheart,
   I'm after a prize to-night,
But I shall be back with the yellow gold
   before the morning light;

Yet, if they press me sharply,
　　and harry me through the day,
Then look for me by moonlight,
　　Watch for me by moonlight,
I'll come to thee by moonlight,
　　though hell should bar the way."

He rose upright in the stirrups.
　　He scarce could reach her hand,
But she loosened her hair in the casement.
　　His face burnt like a brand
As the black cascade of perfume
　　came tumbling over his breast;
And he kissed its waves in the moonlight,
　　　　(O, sweet black waves in the moonlight!)
Then he tugged at his rein in the moonlight,
　　and galloped away to the west.

He did not come in the dawning.
He did not come at noon;

And out of the tawny sunset,
    before the rise of the moon,
When the road was a gypsy's ribbon,
    looping the purple moor,
A red-coat troop came marching —
        Marching — marching —
King George's men came marching,
    up to the old inn-door.

They said no word to the landlord.
　　They drank his ale instead.
But they gagged his daughter, and bound her,
　　to the foot of her narrow bed.
Two of them knelt at her casement,
　　with muskets at their side!
There was death at every window;
　　　　And hell at one dark window;
For Bess could see, through her casement,
　　the road that *he* would ride.

They had tied her up to attention,
    with many a sniggering jest.
They had bound a musket beside her,
    with the muzzle beneath her breast!
"Now, keep good watch!" and they kissed her.
    She heard the doomed man say —
*Look for me by moonlight;*
    *Watch for me by moonlight;*
*I'll come to thee by moonlight,*
    *though hell should bar the way!*

She twisted her hands behind her;
    but all the knots held good!
She writhed her hands till her fingers
    were wet with sweat or blood!
They stretched and strained in the darkness,
    and the hours crawled by like years,
Till, now, on the stroke of midnight,
      Cold, on the stroke of midnight,
The tip of one finger touched it!
    The trigger at least was hers!

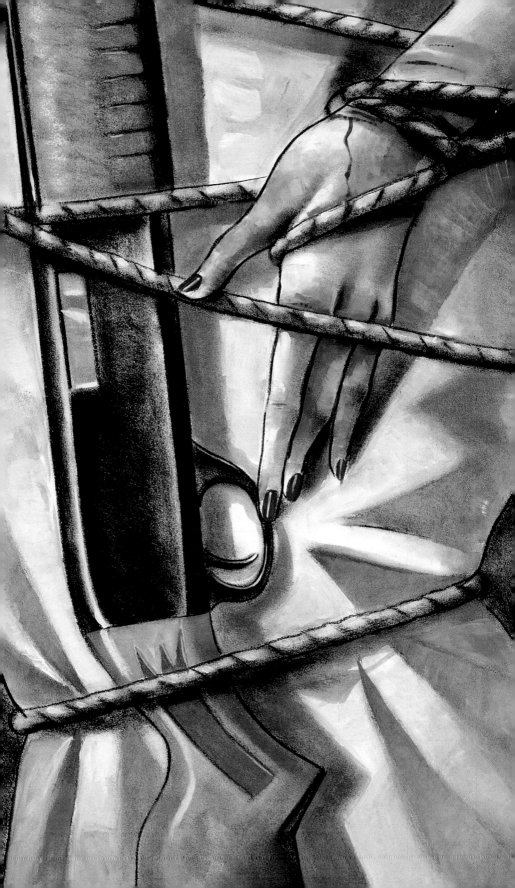

The tip of one finger touched it
    She strove no more for the rest.
Up, she stood up to attention,
    with the muzzle beneath her breast.
She would not risk their hearing;
    she would not strive again;
For the road lay bare in the moonlight;
      Blank and bare in the moonlight;
And the blood of her veins, in the moonlight,
    throbbed to her love's refrain.

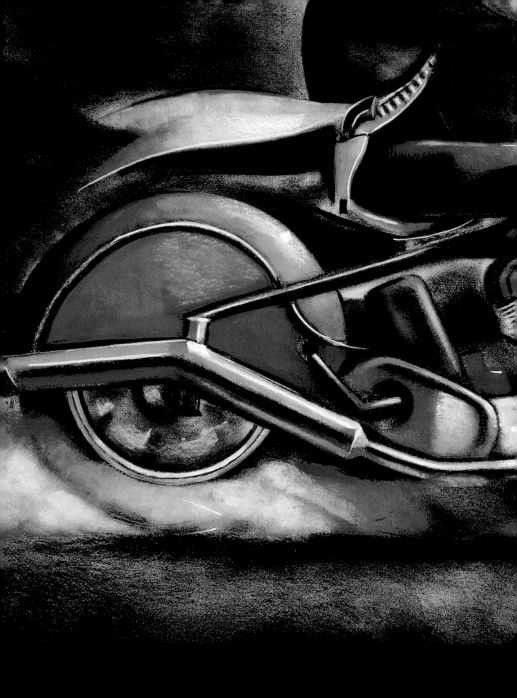

*Tlot-tlot; tlot-tlot!* Had they heard it?
　　The horse-hoofs ringing clear;
*Tlot-tlot, tlot-tlot,* in the distance?
　　Were they deaf that they did not hear?

Down the ribbon of moonlight,
over the brow of the hill,
The highwayman came riding —
Riding — riding —
The red-coats looked to their priming!
She stood up, straight and still.

*Tlot-tlot,* in the frosty silence!

    *Tlot-tlot,* in the echoing night!

Nearer he came and nearer.

    Her face was like a light.

Her eyes grew wide for a moment;

    she drew one last deep breath,

Then her finger moved in the moonlight,
     Her musket shattered the moonlight,
Shattered her breast in the moonlight
    and warned him — with her death.

He turned. He spurred to the west;
    he did not know who stood
Bowed, with her head o'er the musket,
    drenched with her own blood!
Not till the dawn he heard it,
    and his face grew grey to hear
How Bess, the landlord's daughter,
      The landlord's black-eyed daughter,
Had watched for her love in the moonlight,
    and died in the darkness there.

Back, he spurred like a madman,
    shouting a curse to the sky,
With the white road smoking behind him
    and his rapier brandished high.
Blood-red were his spurs in the golden noon;
    wine-red was his velvet coat;

When they shot him down on the highway,
Down like a dog on the highway,
And he lay in his blood on the highway,
with a bunch of lace at his throat.

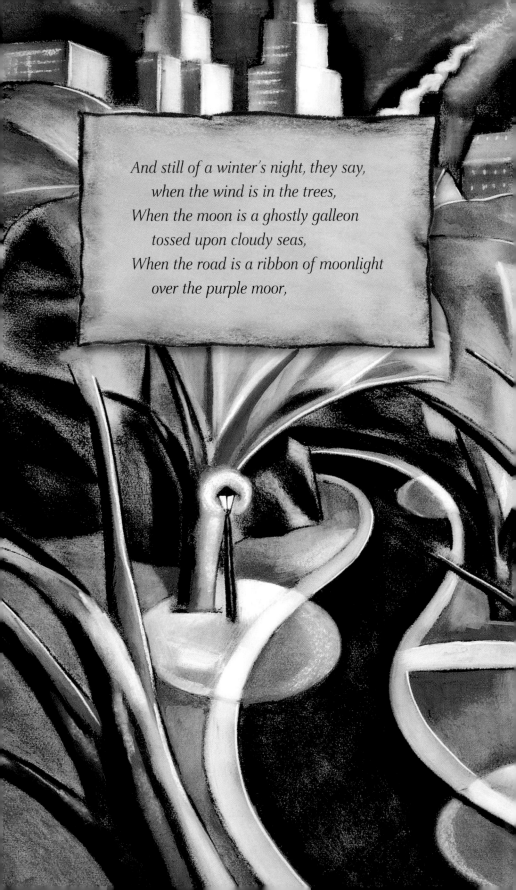

And still of a winter's night, they say,
    when the wind is in the trees,
When the moon is a ghostly galleon
    tossed upon cloudy seas,
When the road is a ribbon of moonlight
    over the purple moor,

*A highwayman comes riding —*
*Riding — riding —*
*A highwayman comes riding,*
*up to the old inn-door.*

*Over the cobbles he clatters and clangs*
*in the dark inn-yard.*
*He taps with his whip on the shutters,*
*but all is locked and barred.*
*He whistles a tune to the window,*
*and who should be waiting there*
*But the landlord's black-eyed daughter,*
*Bess, the landlord's daughter,*
*Plaiting a dark red love-knot*
*into her long black hair.*

# ALFRED NOYES

Although his popularity has waned over the years, Englishman Alfred Noyes (1880–1958) was one of the most celebrated poets of his time. While he was an undergraduate at Oxford, his first book of poems, *The Loom of Years* (1902), was praised by respected poets William Butler Yeats and George Meredith. Published and widely reviewed in both Britain and the United States, Noyes also wrote short stories, novels, essays, plays and biographies, producing approximately 60 books during his career. In 1914, he accepted a teaching position at Princeton University, where he taught English literature until 1923. Noyes came back to North America years later, residing in Canada and the United States for much of World War II. In 1949, he returned to Britain; suffering from increasing blindness, he began dictating his work, which he would do for the remainder of his life.

A noted critic of modernist writers such as James Joyce and T.S. Eliot, Noyes was a literary conservative who followed traditional models in the structure and subject of his poetry. The appeal of his poems lies largely in their rhythm and rhyme, melodic and sonorous lines, and memorable refrains, all of which figure prominently in "The Highwayman." Its hypnotic rhythm and Noyes's repetition of words and phrases reminiscent of the galloping pace of the horseman have made it a popular choice for recitation among generations of schoolchildren.

Arguably Noyes's most famous work, "The Highwayman" originally appeared in *Forty Singing Seamen and Other Poems* (1907). This haunting, romantic ballad of doomed love has thrilled readers of all ages since its publication and is considered one of the most beloved poems in the English language. The lovers' tragic fate and the poem's dramatic detail, ghostly atmosphere and vivid imagery also account for its timeless allure. "The Highwayman" is a poem that continues to haunt our imaginations just as the highwayman's spirit lives on, lingering on moonlit winter nights over the purple moor.

# MURRAY KIMBER

For artist Murray Kimber, illustrating "The Highwayman" presented a considerable challenge: How could he bring a new vision to a poem that has been beautifully depicted many times over? Kimber was excited to make this classic poem more relevant to young readers by giving it a modern twist but initially found himself limited by the text's precise historical and visual references. Only when he stepped back from the details did Kimber see the value in telling a parallel story through his art, one inspired by what had initially appealed to him about the poem — the larger theme of the anti-hero struggling against authority. After experimenting with different approaches and settings, he was struck by the idea of an American cops and robbers story. Drawing on his fascination with comic books, gangster movies and film noir, Kimber replaced the horse with a motorcycle, recast King George's soldiers as FBI agents and relocated the action from rural England to the streets of Art Deco–era New York City.

Though the images reflect an updated urban scene, Kimber's art still powerfully evokes the poem's haunting spirit. His cool blues and grays capture the moonlit winter night's moody atmosphere, while the warm browns suggest the passion of the lovers' enduring bond. Striking, sophisticated and stylish, Kimber's modern, cinematic vision breathes new life into Noyes's classic and will electrify a whole new generation of readers.

A graduate of The Alberta College of Art & Design, Murray Kimber has received critical acclaim and numerous awards for his work. The illustrations for his first picture book, *Josepha*, won him the prestigious Governor General's Award for Illustration, Canada's highest literary honor. He also illustrated *Fern Hill*, *The Wolf of Gubbio* and, most recently, *Ancient Voices*. In addition to children's books, Kimber does commercial artwork for an impressive list of international clients and has held several exhibitions of his original paintings. He lives in Nelson, British Columbia, with his wife and daughter.

To Mom and Dad for having the good sense not to dissuade
their young sons from spending hours reading comic books.
My loving thanks to Kari and Isabella. My respectful thanks to
Tara and Karen, who will wince with the knowledge that each
painting took an average of 40 days to complete — M.K.

The illustrations for this book were rendered in
charcoal, conté and acrylic on paper.

The text was set in

_Streamline,_ BODEGA SANS and Celeste

KCP Poetry is an imprint of Kids Can Press

Text © Alfred Noyes 1913, renewed 1941
Illustrations © 2005 Murray Kimber

Kids Can Press acknowledges the financial support of the Government of Ontario,
through the Ontario Media Development Corporation's Ontario Book Initiative;
the Ontario Arts Council; the Canada Council for the Arts; and the
Government of Canada, through the BPIDP, for our publishing activity.

| Published in Canada by | Published in the U.S. by |
|---|---|
| Kids Can Press Ltd. | Kids Can Press Ltd. |
| 29 Birch Avenue | 2250 Military Road |
| Toronto, ON  M4V 1E2 | Tonawanda, NY  14150 |

www.kidscanpress.com

Edited by Tara Walker
Designed by Karen Powers
Printed and bound in China

This book is smyth sewn casebound.

CM 05  0 9 8 7 6 5 4 3 2 1

**National Library of Canada Cataloguing in Publication Data**

Noyes, Alfred, 1880–1958
The highwayman / Alfred Noyes ; with illustrations by Murray Kimber.

(Visions in poetry)

ISBN 1-55337-425-8

1. Brigands and robbers — Juvenile poetry. 2. Children's poetry, English.
I. Kimber, Murray, 1964– II. Title. III. Series.

PR6027.O8H5 2005     j821'.912     C2004-902478-7

Kids Can Press is a _Corus_™ Entertainment company